It's a
Choice

Behind the Scenes at the YMCA

Bill Lamia

ISBN: 1540852547
ISBN 13: 9781540852540
Library of Congress Control Number: 2016920358
CreateSpace Independent Publishing Platform
North Charleston, South Carolina

Inspired by UBU

Contents

Foreword

I LIVE IN a town to which I have little connection. I'm not from here. I moved here because it was affordable, and mostly what binds me to the community is my mortgage. The neighbors and I are cordial; we wave, but we have little in common beyond a street address. A few days a week, I'm allowed to work from home, and I start those blessed days with a twenty-minute drive to the Randolph YMCA, New Jersey, as I did this morning.

I know when I get to the Y on time because Concetta is just finishing up in the locker room, and we can wish each other good day. Manissi was in a rush to get to work today but screeched to a halt when she saw me to give me a big hug and to ask if I was well before continuing her dash out of the locker room. I got myself ready for a workout and headed downstairs.

I stopped in the doorway of the weight room to look for "traffic" on the indoor track. Bob, a senior, was headed around the curve. "Where ya been, stranger?" After chatting with Bob, I spotted Tony at the weight machines and headed that way. I got a big hug, and we shared our news. Tony brought me up to speed on Bethany, who wasn't there today, and made sure I promised to go to the field hockey tryouts, even though we know I have little chance of making the team this time. The first time I wanted to try out, I told Tony and Bethany specifically because I knew they wouldn't let me chicken out. I tried to return the favor when they became qualified to teach spinning—I signed up for their first class, which is much earlier than I generally arrive at the Y, under a fake name so I could surprise them.

Five minutes on the elliptical is my preferred starting point, and I climbed aboard. Jeff called hello and waved from the middle of the weight room. John jokingly greeted me by peering from in between several weight machines. Another fifteen minutes of various warm-up exercises, and I headed upstairs to the basketball gym to make use of the space. But first, I stopped by the front desk, leaned over the edge, and swiped a few tissues from the box I'm not sure I'm allowed to take tissues from. One of the desk ladies looked at me, and I said, "You saw nothing."

She winked and said, "I don't even know what you're talking about."

I headed back down the hall to the gym and ran into Ron, another senior, who asked if I was behaving. "Of course not; I model my behavior after yours!"

Into the basketball gym for shuttle runs. Just when I was thinking to myself that nobody would really notice if I cut this short, Bill, the author of this book, poked his head in the door to commend the "old-school" workout. We high-fived, and I decided I should finish after all. Bill went on his way, and Carlos showed up with his soccer ball. Carlos and his sometime workout partner, Marcello, are two of the fittest men I know and about fifteen years younger than I am. When I was just starting to work out hard, all by myself downstairs in the weight room, they introduced themselves to me and told me to come work out with them. The fact that I was significantly older and significantly less fit than they did not register; they just saw somebody trying really hard and wanted to be supportive. They showed me that I could do much more than I realized.

Finally I'm done, showered, and on my way out the door. I run into Kathy L., who wants to know when I'll be back in abs class; I haven't been in a while. A few steps farther and I meet Kathy F., featured in this book, who asks when we can meet to go over my water-training plan. I tell her that because of this book, I took the tethered swim class, which I'll do again tomorrow. When I arrive home, Anjana, from the YMCA marine-style boot camp fitness class, has texted me photos from the Spartan race many of the boot-campers ran over the weekend. She says they missed me.

That was today. Actually, it was just two hours of today. And I can name many other Y friends whom I did not happen to run into this morning.

For some years, I have been telling people that the YMCA is my true neighborhood. It's the community to which I am connected. When Bill told me about this book and the fact that he wanted to convey to people what a special place the YMCA is, I understood exactly what he meant. But as rich and warm as my own experience has been at the Y, I came to realize through the following pages that I had only scratched the surface of what this YMCA community has to offer to all of us and the important role it is playing in the lives of so many of our neighbors.

You know why it's my choice to come here. Read on for a behind-the-scenes look at the YMCA, and learn why so many others have also made it their choice.

Karen Chambers

YMCA Member

Introduction: Shaving My Head

I'M BALD. NOT entirely bald but also not sold on the comb-over. So in my thirties, I chose to shave it all off completely. I need to shave my head every single morning before work; otherwise, I look a little rough around the edges. Every morning, I lather up my face, my head, and my neck and shave. I shave everything in about three-and-one-half minutes, quickly lather up again, touch it up, rinse it off, and I'm good to go. Oddly enough, a few years ago, I realized that I get my greatest inspiration every morning during those three-and-one-half minutes while I'm shaving my head. My most recent inspiration was to finish this book, and the title, *It's a Choice*, popped into my head—*It's a Choice* because it is a choice. Every single day, I get to choose how I will react to every situation and every person who comes my way. As you'll see, a lot comes my way.

This book has been a project of mine over the last three years. And by "mine," I mean me. I'm the CEO of a YMCA, with the support of my colleague, Kathy, who is the aquatics director at the same Y. I hired Kathy in 2004 because she had a wealth of aquatic experience combined with a fun, easy, and direct personality. Early on in her first year, I made a habit of checking in with her daily to discuss her department, budget, programs, and personnel. After the business portion of our conversations, we would inevitably begin telling short stories about Y members and workday situations that often led to hearty laughter, somber moments, or blank (I can't believe what I just heard) stares. Naturally, we would share these same on-the-job stories with other members and friends outside the Y, and we soon discovered we both always received the same response—"You should write a book." We agreed but also quickly learned that saying you are going to write a book and actually writing a book is similar to saying you are going to get in shape and actually getting in shape. Starting is always the hardest part, and after years of talking about it, I woke up one day, got inspired while I shaved my head, and decided to do it. I figured if friends and family enjoyed our short stories about the Y, then they, and perhaps others, would also enjoy an assortment of stories captured in a book.

We started simply by taking notes and writing rough-draft stories of our experiences as YMCA employees. Kathy would randomly e-mail me her information, and I found the memo pad on my smartphone became ultra-important because, as situations were occurring at the Y in real time or a thought popped into my head, I would click on the phone, jot down a few notes for the book, and revisit the topic at a later date to add the detail. As it turned out, writing helped me remember and embrace the significance of all the different types of people I've met. The truth is that I can become so wrapped up in the business of operating a Y that it's easy to forget why I chose to work at a Y in the first place. My inspiration for sharing these stories is simply to connect you with the characters I've met and to share with you what I've learned. Perhaps, in some small way, it will help you navigate the complexities of life. Quite honestly, our experiences are probably better suited for a sitcom or a movie, but for now, a book will have to do.

The YMCA is so much more than a building with fitness equipment, pools, and basketball courts. The Y is a safe haven and a place to take a mini vacation from all the confusion of politics, traffic, annoying workdays, and daily stress. The Y is a place to heal as well as a place to socialize, energize, and become a better person. Ultimately, and in its simplest form, the Y is about people. Every day and in every way, we deal with people. People in suits and ties, people in workout gear, people in bathing suits, people dressing, people undressing, disabled people, special needs people, all walks of life, all nationalities, and all income levels. We make a choice every day about how we interact with people. It's not a hard job, and it's not an easy job, and in many ways, it's not even a job—it's a life. It's motivating, frustrating, heartwarming, and heartbreaking all within a split second.

The lessons I have learned at the Y have taught me to live simply and to take one day at a time. My mom told me years ago that you learn by listening, not by talking, and somewhere along the line I heeded her advice. I am certain that the wisdom and knowledge that I learned by listening to members of all ages at the Y has helped me avoid many critical mistakes in my work life and personal life. Many of the people in the stories I value as friends, and I consider myself blessed that they are in my life. I think the stories I share, along with the lessons both Kathy and I have learned, could change your life the way they've changed our lives. Or maybe they won't, but either way, it is therapeutic for me to tell you what it's like to work at the Y. For those of you who are YMCA staff or members, you'll be able to relate quickly and will undoubtedly have similar types of stories. For those of you who are not YMCA members, you'll get a glimpse of what the YMCA really is, far beyond the pool, the basketball court, and the weight room that first jump to mind.

1
Looking through a Lens

WHILE THE LITTLE girl was eating her lunch, a bee decided to land inside her soda can for a swim. The little girl took a sip and swallowed the bee, which promptly stung her in the throat. It's summer camp season at the YMCA! The reality of caring for hundreds of children all day five days a week in a summer camp setting can easily become overwhelming.

I'm often asked what my typical day is like. The simple answer is that there is no typical day. As compared to a construction worker who builds a house, hands the homeowner the key, and walks away, there is never a day that I say, "I'm finished." Customer service is only as good as your last interaction with a member; swim lessons and childcare are only as good as your last safe and fun day, respectively; and finances are only as good as your ability to pay the bills. I often say that we are only ever as good as our last ten minutes, and I sincerely mean it because that type of thinking keeps everything in perspective. Positively and negatively, conditions and community needs change fast, and it is our job to respond accordingly. Whoever wrote, "It's never what happens to you; it's always how you respond to it," must have worked at a YMCA.

From my perspective, there are three qualities necessary to be the CEO of a YMCA. You need to be patient, you need to be proactive, and you need to surround yourself with highly qualified professionals. And once you've mastered those skills, you'll need to go back and master them again.

Considering that I am operating a YMCA with well over seventy-five hundred members who have seventy-five hundred different opinions, the need for a significant amount of patience cannot be overstated. The pool water is too hot. The pool water is too cold. The pool water is just right. Please turn up the air conditioner. Please turn down the air conditioner. We need a fan. We don't need a fan. The music is too loud; turn down the volume. Turn up the music volume. I like the music station. I don't like the music station. The locker room is really clean. The locker room is dirty. The steam room is too steamy. We need more steam. The hot tub is too hot. The hot tub is too cold. The lap swimmers want more time in the pool, the basketball players want more time on the courts, the pickleball players want more time in the gymnasium, and babysitting is full. There is no trick to handling these comments; they are all fair and valid observations by members who pay my salary. The moment my response becomes defensive and agitated instead of patient and sincere is the moment I fail.

I learned early on in my Y career that managing reactively is bad and managing proactively is good. As a new YMCA physical education director, I recall my boss pointing out dust on the floors and in the corners of the exercise machines. He swiped the dust with his index finger, looked at me while showing the dust he had collected, and said, "Not clean." I took that to heart, and my personal goal was to make sure that he never said that to me again. I put a plan in place to keep the floors and equipment spotless. A week or so later, my boss toured my department again. He eyeballed the floors and equipment and then walked over to me. I was expecting a compliment because the equipment that he was inspecting was so immaculate that he didn't even have to do the finger test, but to my surprise he said, "You need to look up because the ceiling fans are full of dust." I was crushed. But he was right. That was the day I figured out that in order to succeed in my career, I needed to try to stay two steps ahead. My boss asked me to clean the floor and equipment, and I did, but that was reactive. I should have been proactive and cleaned the fans, mirrors, windows, and desks in addition to what he originally asked. It's one of the most important management lessons I've learned, and I do my best to pay the same lesson forward to the staff that I manage.

On a Monday morning, I walked in the back door of the Y, and the first person I bumped into was a member named Carlos. In his broken English he said, "Good morning, Bill! I realized this morning why I come here five days a week, and it's not because I like to exercise. It's because the staff are so friendly, and they take really good care of me." It is the best compliment I ever received at the Y. Therein lies the greatest challenge of operating a large nonprofit organization with a staff of more than four hundred, the majority of whom are part time. In order for the Y to be successful, I have to have the right employees in the right places. Great staff is essential. I've always purposely surrounded myself with smart, energetic people. It sounds simple, but it's not a perfect science.

I want to be challenged by staff, I want their thoughts and ideas that test the status quo, and I want them to succeed beyond their wildest imagination. My feeling is that if they succeed, then the organization as a whole succeeds.

Consider this: Our summer camp directors are responsible for hundreds of children who, on any given day, may be spread out over all parts of New Jersey and New York on fun field trips. In one day, they may have the first and second graders at a zoo, the third and fourth graders at Dorney Amusement Park, the fifth and six graders rafting down the Delaware River, and the seventh and eighth graders visiting the Empire State Building. The number of things that can go wrong—including things beyond our control—can easily be overwhelming. Patient, proactive, and professional staff is absolutely essential. A typical day at the Y simply does not exist.

Thankfully, a camp counselor was sitting directly across from the little girl who was stung in the throat. She jumped to action, comforted the girl, watched for swelling and lightheadedness, notified the camp director, and called the little girl's parents. Incredibly, by the time the parents arrived, the patient was feeling much better. She went home for the day, checked in with the family doctor, and was back at camp the very next morning.

2
Ashes

WORK OUT, USE the pool, and faint in the hot tub. Repeat. Workout, use the pool, and faint in the hot tub. Kathy had told Ralph many times that she did not want him in the hot tub. He was forever sneaking in when the staff wasn't looking, so Kathy put up a "wanted" poster right next to the hot tub with his face on it and the following message: "If you see this man, turn him in immediately to the aquatics authorities. He is unarmed and dangerous to himself." Ralph had many friends, and Kathy convinced them to turn him in. Her conversation with Ralph went like this:

"Hey, Ralph, if I catch you in the hot tub again, then I'll have to throw you out of the Y."

"What do you mean?"

"You know what I mean. I can't keep picking you up off the floor. It's not healthy for you. Really, Ralph, what if you split your head open on the hard tile pool deck when you faint and fall? Then what?"

"Hey, Kathy, here's how I look at it. I've had a great life. What would be better than dying in the arms of your best friends in a place that you love?"

"Never going to happen on my watch, Ralph. And besides, I don't want the paperwork. Stay out of the hot tub."

Ralph kept sneaking into the hot tub. Ralph was an eighty-five-year-old YMCA member who arrived every day at 5:30 a.m. He first learned how to e-mail when he was in his eighties, and he e-mailed Kathy every day. She still has the first e-mail he ever sent, which he thought he was sending anonymously: "If you could just lower the TVs in the cardio room, our necks wouldn't hurt so much. Also please raise the hooks in the lockers in the men's locker room; our pants keep falling off them." It was signed "The boys." How raising the hooks in the locker room would prevent their pants from falling off remains a mystery. She should have asked him when she had the chance. Ralph passed away at the age of ninety-one. It turns out that his final wish was for a group of us from the Y to spread his ashes over the twelfth hole at his favorite golf course. We were honored. We met one beautiful and picturesque spring morning: Kathy, our YMCA board president, four of Ralph's dearest friends, and me. In fact, Ralph could have named fifty close friends at the Y to spread his ashes, and all fifty would have been honored to do so. Ralph simply had that certain intangible personality trait that resulted in an enormous number of friendships. Whether it was his sincerity, humor, laughter, or self-confidence, I'm not sure—but I do know that he was special. While we all knew Ralph from different angles and all had different running jokes and conversations going, there is no question that it was the Y that was the bond that connected us on this day.

Arriving at the golf course, we jumped into three golf carts and proceeded to the twelfth hole. Kathy rode with Kim, Ralph's favorite golf companion. Kim was a character in her own right. Unbeknownst to Kathy, she drove like a maniac, and as soon as she was in the cart, Kim put her foot to the floor and sped off as fast as a golf cart could possibly go toward the twelfth hole. The twelfth hole on this course has a spectacular scenic view; I could understand why Ralph had selected this location. We were looking out on a beautiful vista covered in dew on this exquisite spring morning, each of us prepared with the words that would best honor our dear friend. Suddenly, up drove the golf course attendant, yelling at us: "Hey, what the hell are you doing? There's a tournament today. You can't be here!"

It turned out that our board president knew Sam, the golf course attendant. "Hey, Sam. How's it going? Look, we have permission to be out here; we're honoring the passing of a dear friend by spreading—"

Sam cut him right off. "Look, you have to get out of here, and I really don't care what you're doing. Make it fast."

While this one-sided argument was going on, we turned around to see one of Ralph's dear friends frantically dumping Ralph's ashes onto a small hill behind us. There was a slight breeze, so the ashes were creating a human ash mini-dust storm. He finished, put the lid back on the box, put the box in the back of the golf cart, and said, "Come on, let's get out of here!" No stories, no endearing words about what a wonderful man Ralph was, and no prayers. Just a quick ash dump from a box and a "let's get out of here."

Ralph was a character right up until the moment his dearest friends honored his last wishes. Just as he had told Kathy at the YMCA hot tub, "What would be better than dying in the arms of your best friends in a place that you love?"

3
The Best

HE GREW UP an orphan and died in a nursing home with Alzheimer's disease.

It started simply. He would misplace his YMCA keys, forget where he parked his car, or begin discussions on irrelevant topics. From time to time, and for no apparent reason, he would get short and angry with me. Many noticed a change in Ernie, but we always stayed on the side of caring and compassion. Ernie was in the early stages of dementia by the time he was seventy-five.

Ernie was about seventy years old when he approached me one summer for a job working in the fitness area. He was one of those seventy-year-olds who was in terrific shape, had high energy, and a great spirit. I did not have any immediate openings, but I told him to come see me the day after Labor Day.

Ernie knocked at my door the day after Labor Day. I hired him on the spot. I didn't have an immediate shift for him to cover, but I wanted his spirit on my staff team, and I was impressed that he followed up precisely as we had discussed. As far as I'm concerned, a job can be taught, but Ernie's energy, enthusiasm, and attention to detail are innate personality traits that I knew would be of great value to the Y. He started as a substitute in case an employee called out sick and, as luck would have it, within a few weeks, our opening shift, beginning at 5:30 a.m., became vacant, and Ernie landed his own shift—Monday through Friday from 5:30 a.m. until 9:00a.m. To this day, Ernie was the best part-time employee the YMCA has ever had. "No problems, only solutions" was his motto. He was always fifteen minutes early for his 5:30 a.m. shift, knew everybody by name, and had enthusiasm second to none. He set the bar extremely high for all the YMCA staff. As the years went by, I grew close to Ernie, as did many YMCA members. He wasn't just an employee; he was a dear friend to many. And then odd things began to happen.

I was with Ernie every step of the way as his son placed him in a nursing home on the Alzheimer's wing. Walking with Ernie in the hospital hallways and lounge areas was sad and, quite honestly, shocking. The hallways were lined with seniors whose bodies were intact but whose minds were gone. They would walk, sit, or stand and wobble in the hallways, and initially, Ernie looked like a rock star compared to them. I was adamant with whoever would listen that Ernie did not belong on the Alzheimer's wing. I was wrong. I'd visit Ernie three times a week and always on weekends. Watching the progression and the downward spiral of Alzheimer's was incredibly sad. It wasn't long before Ernie was just like the rest of the people in the hall on that wing: he'd walk, sit, stand, wobble, and mumble. Ernie was no longer Ernie.

It was an incredibly touching experience for me to watch this once-great YMCA representative slowly fading and drifting to his death. Most of the people at his funeral were YMCA members and staff, and I recall the pictures that surrounded his coffin: Ernie smiling and surrounded by YMCA members, who were smiling too. Although I hired Ernie to work in the fitness room, his real contribution at the YMCA was in the friendships and relationships he offered the rest of the staff and Y members. Experiences like this keep my life simple and in perspective. It also serves as a reminder about what it is we do at the YMCA. Done right, the YMCA is never about buildings, equipment, treadmills, or pools; it's about people like Ernie and the relationships they forge.

4
Ted

TED MAY OR may not have been a dear friend of mine. I kind of think he was. At least he was to me.

One thing that we had in common was our passion for fishing. When it comes to old-time, experienced fishermen, I am eager to learn, so over the years, Ted and I had great fishing conversations. One hot ninety-degree day in August, he took me trout fishing to one of his favorite spots on the Paulinskill River in New Jersey. I just knew going in that there was no chance in hell that either of us was going to catch any trout in August. Trout are cold-water fish. Most streams in New Jersey get very low, and the water is too warm to hold trout in the summertime. I humored him anyway and went along for the ride. He gave me his old fishing pole and a couple of dozen mealworms and put me in "his" spot. Within a half hour, I had caught four trout—two brookies and two browns. OK, I admit, he knew more than I did about fishing. We fished together about ten times over the next two summers, and each and every time we caught fish. In fact, to this day, many of his old favorite spots are now my favorite spots.

I won't tell you about the longest fish that got away, but I will tell that I believe Ted holds the record for the longest grudge.

Ted's second passion was gambling in Atlantic City, Vegas, and just about anywhere else that gambling was legal. He and I organized a YMCA senior-citizens bus trip to Atlantic City as a fundraiser for the Y. It cost twenty dollars for the trip, and upon arrival, you received ten dollars back for the slot machines. The morning of the trip, another long-time senior friend of ours was feeling ill just before takeoff and decided not to go, so I did the right thing—I refunded his money and sent him home to get well.

Ted was furious that I refunded the money and literally stopped talking to me for the next seven years, which turned out to be the rest of his life. A few months before he passed, I saw Ted in the hallway at the Y, and he finally acknowledged me with an awkward glance and a smirk—but still no words. Ted passed away soon after, so that encounter turned out to be the last time I ever saw him.

Years later, I got the news that Ted's wife had passed too.

Eight months after that, I was notified that Ted had left the YMCA $300,000 in his will. Maybe that's why he gave me a smirk the last time I saw him.

When the executor of Ted's will gave me the check he said, "Did you know Ted?"

I said, "Yes, he was a good friend of the Y's."

He said, "I worked with Ted. He was a great guy, but he could really hold a grudge!"

5
Bob

A SIMPLE HELLO can go in a thousand different directions.

I met Bob in the cardio room at the Randolph YMCA. My simple "Hello, how was your workout?" fostered one of the most meaningful friendships I've ever had. I soon learned that Bob had been a YMCA member at several different Ys for nearly sixty years, and it all began at the Portland YMCA in Maine. He told me quite often that the YMCA was a lifesaver for him, especially as a young child from a broken home. It's where he made his best friends, it's where mentors helped guide him, and most importantly, he'd say, "It's where I learned to play basketball." Bob quickly got involved at our YMCA in Randolph, New Jersey. Soon after I met Bob, I received a call from the front desk while in my office: "Bob and his wife, Mary, would like to see you in the lobby." I strolled down to the lobby, and there were Bob and Mary, sitting in a booth talking to a group of Y friends. I sat across from him and joined the conversation.

Bob handed me a check and simply said, "If a kid or family can't afford a Y membership, then please use this money to pay for it so that they have an opportunity to come to the Y like I did." Bob understood the Y. I invited Bob to be part of the Y's men's club—a group of World War II veterans who socialized with and volunteered for the YMCA in a variety of ways. Nicknamed "The Y's Guys," we all enjoyed meeting for breakfast each month for many years.

One day after breakfast, Bob handed me a check and said, "If ever a veteran would like to join your YMCA, then please put this toward their membership." I'm not sure when it started, but quite a few people at the Y called Bob the "Mayor." It came about because Bob loved talking to people and seemed to know just about everyone. There were times when he would enter the YMCA, and it would take nearly an hour for him to go from the front desk to the men's locker room simply because he knew so many people and had so many conversations on the way.

Bob passed away when he was eighty-four. When I think of Bob, I think of the expression "pay it forward"; that is simply what Bob had a habit of doing—"I learned it at the Y," he'd say. Years before he passed away, Bob and

Mary dedicated a large engraved stone that sits at the front entrance of the Randolph YMCA and quotes Aesop: "No act of kindness, no matter how small, is ever wasted." It is the perfect message in the perfect location.

And it all started with a simple hello.

6
Luis

LUIS IS IN his late sixties. He's hunched over, walks very slowly with the help of a walker, and has a significant speech impediment as if he had a stroke. He is very hard to understand unless you take the time to focus on his speech pattern. When you do get to know him, you find that he is simply a kind, gentle, and positive person. He is always gracious and always has a joke or two despite his slurred speech and legs that don't work. He works out extremely hard—always telling me that his goal is to walk without the walker. Unfortunately, it's obvious that his condition will probably only get worse. The one thing that I will always remember about Luis is that each and every time I say good-bye, he always says, in his slow, slurred speech, "Have a nice day." Considering the source, those four words always brighten my day.

After I spend time with Luis, I am always left a bit confused.

Why is Luis a kind, gentle, and positive guy? He can hardly talk or walk; consequently, he can't work or do many of the simple things many of us take for granted. Yet, day in and day out, he gives off the most positive energy.

Why are some people so negative by nature? I interact with hundreds of people a week, and one thing that I have noticed is that there are many people who seem to have "everything"—healthy children, healthy marriage, money, friends, nice house, good job—yet they appear to walk through life miserable and negative each day. Not mean, just negative.

I'm not the judge, and the questions I pose may be one of life's greatest mysteries. I'm not sure Luis knows how much he taught me with so few words. But I'm not surprised that I met Luis at the Y; somehow, his type seems to find us.

7
Alberto

HIS HOUSE IS old. His furniture is old. He is old. Alberto is an eighty-seven-year-old who has one son and lives alone. He lives simply and does not have a lot, but he is so generous to so many people. He brings home-made wine to his foot doctor, cookies to Herb, pigs' feet to Bonnie, ham to Anne, hot dogs to Esteban, and vodka to me. Sometimes he gave out what I call hard goods—old mugs, plates, forks, and spoons—to friends at the Y.

I call Alberto the father of functional training. He was doing balancing and functional exercises before balancing and functional exercises were cool. He actually created an apparatus where he was able to balance a ball on his head and walk in the shallow end of the pool. I also saw him with a ball on his head on many occasions in the locker room, in the hallway, and on the indoor track. At times, he would simply be sitting in the lobby with the ball on his head. Apparently, he had foot problems from diabetes, or as he would call it, "sugar," and the balancing exercises helped him. It actually makes sense.

Alberto was one of a kind and prone to saying some incredibly perceptive things:

- Alberto on feeding the hungry: "I can solve the damn hunger problem in New Jersey [meaning feeding the homeless]. Give the prisoners two meals a day instead of three, and give the homeless the meal that's left over."
- Alberto on pregnant women: "They should not be allowed to park in handicapped parking close to the building. Their doctors always say to get some exercise, and walking is the best exercise. They should park farthest from the building."

I would call and check on Alberto often, especially if I did not see him at the Y. If I forgot to call him, then he would call me. For years, his voicemail message to me was always the same: "Hey, what, are you mad at me? I haven't heard from you today! If I'm in the toilet, then leave it on the machine."

8
Return on Investment

CLYDE IS LEGENDARY.

I would visit him often, and I especially remember my winter visits. He'd be sitting in his rocking chair wearing three flannel shirts and a wool hat, because oil was expensive, and he didn't want to turn on the heat. Every once in a while, he would ask me to "turn on the oil burner for a few minutes." Each and every time I visited, he would give me a tour of his house, room by room. Clyde moved slowly, always turning the light switch on as we entered each room and off as we exited each room so he would not spend too much on electricity. Clyde had an interior painting project that seemed to last for years because he would use only a two-inch paintbrush; a roller wasted too much paint. After the tour inside, we inevitably walked outside so he could show me his tomato gardens. Each garden was lined with blocks and stones that he had picked up in various locations over the years. All the stones were mismatched, but, as he explained, they were free.

Clyde was on the board of directors at the YMCA for more than thirty years. Each month, we had a board meeting that began at 6:00p.m. I would arrive at Clyde's house at 3:00p.m. in order to get him there on time. Meetings always lasted about an hour longer when Clyde was present. In his unique, raspy voice, he'd love to talk about all his brilliant ideas, and "bless your soul" if you disagreed with him. He would simply continue to talk and talk and talk until you finally gave in.

One day in November, while Clyde was walking to his mailbox, he fell and broke his hip. He was rushed to the hospital. I visited him often, and it was then I realized that he didn't have any family. Ninety-year-old Clyde had outlived everyone. It wasn't long after he was brought to the hospital that poor old Clyde passed away. The YMCA was in Clyde's will. He had left us $3.5 million, along with his house and all the contents. It is the classic story of the millionaire next door. Legend has it that Clyde was a shop teacher in the public schools and never made more than $26,000 a year in his life. Apparently, he bought bank stocks for many years, and it was that, plus his frugality, through which he made his fortune. We had heard that Clyde had changed his will late in his life to include the Y, but we didn't know the amount.

When I tell people this story, they can't fathom the type of return that Clyde received simply by investing in bank stocks. They can't fathom why he lived so frugally. Although that return is significant and a financial success story in and of itself, it pales in comparison to the everlasting way that he's changed lives long after his passing. Clyde loved the YMCA, and his money built our warm-water pool and our family center. To this day, thousands of families, children, adults, and seniors continue to benefit from Clyde's extraordinary gift. When I think of a true return on investment, I think of Clyde.

9
Alex

ALLELUIA! ALLELUIA! THE good Lord will come!

One man singing church songs rang loud and true as I entered the men's locker room. I've heard the songs for years; it's Alex standing in front of the mirror in just a towel, shaving and singing.

Alex has one of those incredible memories that you only read about. He remembers snow days from third grade, knows every YMCA room schedule and program offering to the minute, and is a risk-management expert. He is not shy about sharing his knowledge with anyone at anytime, yet he is well respected by all, and, to many staff and members, he's a friend.

What members don't know is that Alex is also my secret weapon. Because he knows every YMCA rule, he makes sure I know when members are not following them. Quite honestly, he knows the rules better than I do. Between

1:00 p.m. and 4:00 p.m. every day, Alex is in the house, and he's watching. If you track water into the dry area of the locker room, leave soap on the shower floor, don't sit on a towel in the sauna, don't shower before you go in the pool, mess with the thermostat in the steam room, bring a newspaper in the sauna, or clip your nails and leave them on the floor, then he'll know, and then I'll know. Don't mess with Alex.

10
Mr. Pickleball

IT'S NOT EVERY day that you receive a phone call from the Pickleball Ambassador: "Hi. I'm the Pickleball Ambassador for Morris County, and I'd like to know if your Y is interested in starting a program?"

"Pickleball? What's pickleball?" I asked, as I reached to my computer to Google "pickleball" midconversation. I found nine million websites about pickleball, so I said, "Let's meet!"

Six months later, the YMCA had three official indoor pickleball courts and 189 pickleball players and growing. The first rule of business is to give them what they want; consequently, future outdoor pickleball courts are planned. Pickleball at the Y was an incredible success story simply because of one person's passion. On the outside, it appeared that Mr. Pickleball's obsession was simply to play pickleball. But I was fortunate enough to get to know him and learned that he had an entirely different motivation for calling me that day. It turns out that he really enjoys bringing people together in a fun, healthy environment. Mr. Pickleball knows everyone by name, everyone's skill set, and everyone's personality. He's kind, energetic, and fun. People like him. He believes individuals can draw great personal strength from groups that are focused on positive and healthy activities. Pickleball was simply a vehicle to do that. Mr. Pickleball is a perfect match for the YMCA.

11
BBQ

IT WAS A classic family barbecue: folding lawn chairs, hamburgers, hotdogs, music, Budweiser, and kids running around with water pistols and water balloons. I fell into conversation with Jim, our host's father, a man maybe in his early seventies. We began talking about the YMCA, and the conversation steered toward all the different challenges of operating a nonprofit organization. It turns out that he was very familiar with the Y, and he had a lot of fun stories to share from his childhood experiences there. Sometime during the course of our conversation, I mentioned to Jim that I was dealing with a tough situation where the drop ceiling over our main YMCA pool was failing, and I needed it repaired quickly; otherwise, I would have to close the pool altogether. It was a $100,000 repair, and I was struggling to come up with both the money and a contractor who could do the work right away.

Fast-forward three days. I'm in my front yard cutting the lawn, and Jim, the man from the picnic, pulls up in front of my house in an old Buick. I turn off my lawnmower, he gets out of his car, we make small talk, and he hands me an envelope. It was a $60,000 check and a contractor's business card. He told me to get the project started. I was speechless. As it happens, Jim had been a successful businessman, and he was happy to make the contribution. He also taught me the only three fundraising rules that I'll ever need to know.

- Rule one: people give only to what they feel connected to. If your prospective donor's heart is not connected to your mission, then you will not get a donation. Weeks later and after the pool ceiling had been repaired, Jim shared with me his connection to the Y and the reason for the donation. He had been a part of this particular Y since he was a child. He remembers sneaking into the gymnasium for basketball games with his friends, losing the YMCA youth basketball championship game, and meeting some of his best friends, including his future wife, at the YMCA. Although he stayed in town after graduating college, busy workdays took him away from regular attendance at the Y. As he aged and his career grew, he stayed connected by contributing to the Y financial assistance fund. The financial assistance fund assures that no child or family is turned away from the Y because of their financial situation. It is the essence of our nonprofit status. Jim is connected because the Y played a significant role in his childhood. As he put it, "Naturally, we were his number one charity." I never knew.

- Rule two: people give to people, not places. Donors give only to passionate people who represent an organization they really believe in. Jim sensed that I was passionate about the Y and especially about the immediate challenge of fixing the pool ceiling. Unbeknownst to me, he was wealthy and incredibly generous.

- Rule three: there are a lot of surprises. Without even knowing it, I had planted a seed with Jim, and it germinated in three days. The very last thing that I was thinking about while I was mowing my lawn was receiving a large donation to repair the pool ceiling. But it happened, and the Y was better for it.

12
Above, Not Below

ONE DAY ABOUT midday, when I was having a cup of coffee, eighty-eight-year-old George stopped by for a chat. He enjoyed sharing his wisdom with me, and I enjoyed listening. That day, he told me that being healthy is really quite simple: "If you want to feel good, then help someone else." After he left, I had a "duh" moment. It's so obvious that most people equate being healthy with low body fat, low cholesterol, low resting heart rate, a balanced diet, and a beautiful body. I maintain that those areas are a small part of the equation.

George is slightly overweight, is probably on cholesterol medication, has had open-heart surgery, and enjoys cake with his coffee every day. He's also one of the healthiest people I know. He's simply one of those people who makes others feel good when they're around him. He attracts friends who are young and old and from all walks of life. When he is listening to you, it's apparent that he really cares about you. His daily routine is simple: he wakes up early, comes to the Y to exercise, and spends the rest of the day volunteering for a variety of nonprofits, including those that serve the underprivileged, veterans, and people with special needs. When he's not volunteering, he's with his family. I've known George for years, and by no means has he had an easy life. In fact, considering his life's challenges, he has every reason to be a grumpy old man, yet he chooses the complete opposite. At eighty-eight years old, he is, to me, a picture of health. He's what I'd want to be when I grow old. So next time you see someone who has a beautiful body, can run a marathon, and do twenty pull-ups, it doesn't necessarily mean they're healthy. It simply means they have a beautiful body, can run a marathon, and do twenty pull-ups.

George taught me that health is defined by what's above your shoulders, not below them. If you want to feel good, then choose to help others. It's a choice.

13
Scraping Gum

THE BEST PERSONAL financial advice I ever received was from a guy named Mark who scraped gum off the floor for a living. He owned a cleaning company, and although he cleaned mostly during nonbusiness hours, he always checked in with his customers during the day. Mark always moved really fast and always had a scraper on his belt. Everywhere he walked in the Y, if there was something on the floor that needed to be scraped, then he found it, and he scraped it. "Scraping floors," he'd say, "makes a great impression on your customer because it gives a constant visual that you care about the cleanliness of the building."

Mark taught me about dollar-cost averaging. Dollar-cost averaging is the technique of buying a fixed dollar amount of a particular investment on a regular schedule, regardless of the share price. More shares are purchased when prices are low, and fewer shares are bought when prices are high. You can check Google for more information on why it's a smart way to invest, but that's not the point. Mark was smart; maybe even a genius, but you'd never know it by your first impression. I never saw him dressed in anything more than an old pair of jeans and a T-shirt, except in the winter when he wore a flannel shirt.

At the Y, almost everyone in the building has on shorts and a T-shirt. Their expensive cars are outside, and their thousand-dollar suits are at home. Even a brain surgeon looks like a normal Jane when wearing workout clothes. Suits and ties and fancy cars can be intimidating, and gym shorts and T-shirts are not.

No question about it, the Y is the great human equalizer.

14
My Three Most Inspirational Moments

I NEVER MET anyone as tall as Kevin, and I certainly never met anyone as tall as Kevin who played Division I basketball with one arm. He stood six feet eleven inches, and quite honestly, I barely noticed he was missing a limb because I couldn't get past how tall he was. As Kevin and I toured the Y facility, I noticed he had a certain charisma. As intimidating as his size was, he naturally drew people into conversation in a fun and sincere way. Kevin's personal story of overcoming adversity to become the first one-armed Division I basketball player on scholarship in the country is as inspirational as it gets.

By chance, I was introduced to Kevin through a long-time YMCA member and close friend. He had told me that Kevin was looking for a place to do a basketball clinic for children born with one arm, the same condition that he had, and asked if we could host the event at the YMCA. Honestly, I didn't even know that condition existed, but I was thrilled that he asked and was happy to help.

I recall meeting the parents and children as they entered the lobby to check in for the clinic. Perfect, young children with one arm, the same condition as Kevin. I was a bit overwhelmed at first, but I found immediate comfort in the fact that they were all so capable, happy, and enthusiastic about meeting Kevin and participating in the basketball clinic. All participants brought a friend, and brothers and sisters were encouraged to join in as well. Kevin had a natural ability to connect with people, but he especially enjoyed sharing his talents and inspirational story with young people.

The basketball gym lit up with laughter, squeaky sneakers, and sideline conversations among the families, many of whom already knew one another. For three hours, Kevin delivered as advertised: extraordinary with the kids, inspirational and sincere.

I met a father who drove eighty miles that morning to attend the clinic, and he summed up the day perfectly when he said to me,"All these kids certainly face a unique challenge, but the truth is, one arm or two, we all do. Thanks for bringing us together."

By the time it was over, I was a better person.

• • •

It was my first year as a Y employee. I was the guy who organized and taught all the youth programs in the gymnasium. Late afternoon on this particular day, the aquatics director asked me to assist with a new member, Kim, whose family had just joined the Y, and they wanted her to learn how to swim. It was an odd request considering I had never taught a swim lesson, and we already had a program in place for new beginner swimmers. Then I was told that eight-year-old Kim was born completely blind and had never been in the water. They needed my muscle to assist on the pool deck.

I was really nervous because I had never worked with a blind person before. It is hard to fathom being blind, let alone all the other challenges that would bring. Kim held my arm as we both walked alongside the pool toward the pool stairs. I slowly made a right turn with her and guided her step-by-step down the stairs, into the water, and toward the two swim instructors waiting in the pool. Each step into the water was a brand-new feeling for her, and she would pause at each new water level to process the sensation. Ankle deep, knee deep, waist deep, and then neck deep and into the arms of the swim instructors, who had a firm but gentle and confident grip on her. I'd never seen such a gigantic smile. Kim was in the water for the first time!

It was a brand-new sensation for me as well. It was the first time I sensed that the Y was more than just a fitness center. The innate trust that this new family had in the Y and the immediate caring and respect the aquatics staff had for Kim and her family changed my image of the Y for good.

It wasn't long before Kim became a regular in the pool, participated in swim lessons, and enjoyed family swim with her mom, dad, brother, and sister. This was more than simply learning to swim; I had been apart of their life-changing event.

It wasn't only Kim's life that changed the day.

• • •

Ben is twenty years old, has cerebral palsy, and was unsure about his surroundings when he arrived through the front door of the Y in an automatic wheelchair, accompanied by an aid. You couldn't help but notice his exaggerated reflexes, rigid limbs, and involuntary motions, all the result of his disease. As our two female aquatic rehab specialists met him in the lobby to assist him toward the pool, I could see Ben's excitement.

Ben still arrives in the same wheelchair with the same aid, but there is something different about him. I now see a young man who is calmer, more confident in his abilities, and experiencing the joy of a lot of Y friends. I've watched Ben in the pool many times since that first day, stretched out, more relaxed, exercising, laughing, flirting, and having fun.

When I first met Ben entering the Y, I made the immediate assumption that he is helpless, and we were here to help him. However, I have found time and time again at the Y that often the reverse is true. It is similar to observing a random act of kindness: a young person walking an unstable elderly person across the street or a good deed done when no one is looking. True, goodwill is felt by the recipient, but there is also real satisfaction felt by the person doing the good deed as well as anyone lucky enough to witness it. At its very best, the Y has these moments every day. Yes, our job is to serve, but in serving, if we're tuned in and doing it for the right reasons, then we personally benefit. It's the reason that the Y is such an extraordinary career. Watching our YMCA staff work with Ben made me feel good, and I'm aware that it's moments like this that keep my life in perspective.

15
Old People

MY MOTHER ONCE said that sometimes when you meet an old person you simply think he or she was always old. She's right, and I imagine we are all guilty of it. Consequently, every time I meet an older person, I do all I can to learn about his or her background and listen to his or her wisdom. Some have really boring backgrounds and no wisdom. But many have extraordinary backgrounds and immense wisdom to share. Usually, all you have to do is ask.

Every month, we celebrate the birthdays of all Y members who are eighty or older. At one such birthday party, Stan arrived with a small piece of a propeller from a Japanese kamikaze plane that had bombed the US warship that he was on. He told us the story of how many of his friends died that day. He kept that small piece of propeller as a reminder of how precious life is.

Larry served in the US Army during World War II from 1942 to 1945, was a veteran of the Invasion of Normandy, and fought throughout the European theater until he became a prisoner of war in 1944. He received the Purple Heart in 1945. To know Larry in the hallways of the Y, he was just a pleasant and kind old man trying to keep in shape.

Rich, a retired detective, helped solve one of the most famous and extraordinary kidnapping cases in the state of New Jersey. Rich is unassuming yet one of the most honest and caring people I've ever met. You'd never know his remarkable background unless you asked.

It wasn't until his funeral that I learned that Bert, another Y member, had been placed in a polio isolation hospital at a very young age. In most cases, even parents were not allowed to visit their sick children in the polio ward. Imagine being locked in a sterile isolation room with no indication of the possible outcome of your disease. I never even knew polio isolation hospitals existed. It certainly explains why Bert was such a strong-willed, independent, yet grateful eighty-seven years old when he passed away.

I always ask the same question to each and every older person I meet after learning about his or her astonishing background: "What's the secret to growing old and staying healthy?"

Unequivocally, the answer is to just keep moving forward. Considering the source, it's great advice.

16
Drip-Dry

IT'S AMAZING HOW well you get to know the members at the Y. Incredibly, though, no matter how hard I try, there are some people whose names I just cannot remember. While out to dinner with my wife and other Y people, it became apparent that I was not the only person with this problem. Inevitably, the conversation turned to other Y members, and if we didn't know the member by name, then a quick description was all that was needed, and everybody knew whom we were talking about.

"Drip-dry" was a middle-aged man who would take a shower but never brought a towel. He would walk around the locker room naked, talking with all the members, while he dripped dry. When he didn't have anyone to talk to, he would read a *Time* magazine while standing with one foot on the bench, one foot on the floor, naked, soaking wet, waiting to drip-dry. He did it so often that no one really noticed or cared anymore.

"The guy who always wears the old white T-shirt" was a seemingly poor eighty-nine-year-old member who came to the Y five times a week for as long as I can remember. Although he never really talked to other people, he was very pleasant and very noticeable simply because he was always there. You could say that mystery surrounded him. Interestingly enough, upon his passing, I attended his funeral and learned that he had been married forty-nine years, had seven children, and was an extraordinarily successful businessman.

"Santa" was a member at the Y. Seriously. Santa was a member.

"Scuba" was an overweight gentleman who swam thirty laps every Monday, Wednesday, and Friday at 7:00 a.m. and sometimes on weekends. He was the first person we ever saw use a snorkel to breathe while swimming laps instead of using the traditional freestyle rotary breathing method. To this day, I don't know why the nickname scuba stuck—he probably should have been named "snorkel."

"Sprinter" was an older woman whose entire workout consisted of running really fast, in short bursts, on our indoor track. She was easy to approach and was pleasant to talk to but never initiated a conversation with another member—consequently, it appeared no one ever knew her name.

"Oak tree" was a middle-aged man who never brought a towel to the Y. Why bother? He simply used miles and miles of our paper towels to dry off.

"The lady with the black sweater" was a middle-aged woman who always exercised on the same recumbent bike at the entrance of the cardio room and always had on the same black sweater over her workout gear. It was the type of sweater that you would wear on a cold day in a cabin in the woods. She was always smiling, always friendly, and always wearing her black sweater.

"The Russian vodka guy" had a great philosophy that he shared with me once when I asked how his day was going. He said, "In Russia, they say there is no bad vodka. There is only good vodka and great vodka. And I say the same about every day. There are no bad days, only good days and great days." Apparently, he shared his extraordinary philosophy with many members too.

"The handstand man" was a gentleman in his sixties who would end every workout routine with a five-minute handstand. I always found it amusing when I would walk by. While he was in his handstand position he would say, "Hey, Bill, what's up?"

To which I would always respond, "Hey, handstand man, what's down?"

It is safe to say that YMCAs across the country are really good at embracing and celebrating all people, regardless of their quirks, abilities, disabilities, or the clothes they wear—or don't wear.

17
Super Bowl

ONE DAY, I walked into the men's locker room after my workout, and the first thing I noticed was an extremely overweight, sweaty, fully tattooed new member sitting on the bench in a towel near my locker. I could tell he felt awkward and self-conscious because of his size, so I tried to make him feel comfortable by engaging him in a conversation—something a good YMCA CEO should always do. I asked him about the New York Giants and who he thought was going to win the Super Bowl. "The Giants suck, and how in the hell can anyone pay Eli Manning over ninety-million dollars? Justin Tuck is overrated, Super Bowl Sunday is a waste of time, and all the commercials are terrible," he said in a loud, aggressive tone. By now, everyone in the locker room was staring at us, as he grew angrier and louder by the second.

All I could think about was how to stop the tirade. I cracked a small smile and went to my go-to line: "I wish you would tell me how you really feel." It lightened the mood just enough to end the conversation. He's still a member and became a friend.

18
Fired

EARLY ON IN our careers, no matter what the circumstance, it was always very stressful to fire an employee. The older we get, the more we realize that people usually fire themselves, and all we do is show them the door.

Steve was a great guy who worked as a fitness attendant. Unfortunately, he also had a habit of making inappropriate comments. Firing him was a pleasure, until he walked into the closet of Kathy's office to cry and would not get out.

After having been caught stealing, Jermaine wanted to know why there wasn't some sort of probationary thing that could be done about it. "I'm sorry, Jermaine," Kathy said, "but we don't give you ninety days to take all you can before we let you go."

Stanley was fired because he threatened to "take a guy out" in the parking lot. Kathy actually liked Stan a lot. She gave him a call as soon as she heard about the incident and asked him to come see her right away. He said, "No need to bother with that, Kathy. I'll save you the trouble. Have a nice life."

Kevin failed to show up for three days. He came back expecting business as usual and couldn't believe I fired him.

Sally made threatening comments to her peers about her supervisor. A week before that she had called to say, "Sorry, I'm going to be late. I was just arrested, and I'll be there in a couple of hours." She's another person who Kathy really liked. Sally was totally harmless but could never seem to get her life together.

Barry got into a loud, heated argument with a member who didn't like him. He was a very good staff person who just had a really bad day. I took him out to lunch, gave him some advice, and we parted ways. He thanked me.

Lou was on the maintenance staff and was caught sitting on a lounge chair on the flat roof with an iced tea and a good book, suntanning. Unfortunately for him, I just happened to make my way to the roof to evaluate an HVAC system with a repairman when I caught him. As we parted ways, he wanted to know if I would still give him a good reference.

Fred was a practical joker who rigged my office door so that, when I opened it, hundreds of paper cups would fly around the room. The problem was that I wasn't the one who opened the door first; it was my boss. It scared him senseless, and Fred was fired on the spot. He was the first person I ever saw laughing hysterically while being fired.

19
Things Humans Do

YOU CAN'T MAKE this up. I find humans really entertaining.

Shaving in the hot tub and steam room is forbidden for obvious sanitary reasons. We have big signs that indicate the rule. How can you possibly lie about it when your face is lathered up, you're holding the razor in one hand and the shaving cream in the other, you're on our security camera, and you're looking at me?

Protein is an essential nutrient for building muscle and helps in recovery after a hard workout. Bringing a blender from home and making an after-workout protein shake in the men's locker room while standing naked in front of the mirror talking to your friends is not essential.

Keeping your three-thousand-square-foot house clean is hard. Keeping your sixty-thousand-square-foot YMCA building clean is really hard. I must admit that it annoys me when members purposely leave a dirty two-inch piece of paper towel strategically located under the sauna bench in order to make sure we are cleaning.

You can imagine the chaos when the main sewer drains in the building become clogged and back up. It has happened, and it's because people flush weird things down toilets. We've found T-shirts, screwdrivers, magazines, bathing caps, racquetballs, and mini stuffed animals.

It should go without saying that the proper attire for the pool is a bathing suit. Why, then, was he wearing a cotton T-shirt, cotton sweatshirt, and cotton sweatpants while swimming laps? According to him, it's because he'll get a better workout, and we don't have it in writing that he can't. He won't get a better workout, and we did have it in writing.

You can complain about anything, and I will take it seriously. My job is to deliver extraordinary service, and if you are not happy, then my goal is to make you happy. Although if you complain that there are naked people in the locker room, then there is really not much I can do about it. Humans are allowed to be naked in the locker room.

Some things just should not be done in a public space, such as dyeing your hair. And if you ever do decide to dye your hair in a public space, then you may want to make sure you clean every last drop of dye off the sink area. It's hard to think of anything more disrespectful than finding the remains of a hair-dye job spread out all over the sink, counter, and fixtures.

I'm fully supportive of having clean feet. But please don't place your feet in the sink to wash them. Some things you just can't unsee.

Typically, you wash your body in a shower and your jeans in a washing machine. In order to save water you showered with your jeans on. It's odd, but we do not have a rule that prohibits it. Go for it.

Yes, we have had men and women enter the pool area in nothing but their birthday suits. It's always an accident, and it's always really embarrassing and shocking for the other members and staff.

Yes, we have had women walk into the men's locker room and men walk into the women's locker room to undress, only to realize they are in the wrong one. Most have a sense of humor; some don't.

Proper hydration is really important to maintaining good health, and most Y members understand to bring a water bottle with them. Imagine our surprise when a woman dropped a glass bottle of Kahlúa in the lobby at 9:00a.m. soon after checking in for her morning group-fitness workout.

From time to time, I suspend memberships for not following our rules of conduct. Most times, the member apologizes, fulfills the suspension, and we welcome him or her back as a member in good standing. I was slightly uncomfortable when a member asked if he could bring his priest with him to apologize and "forgive" him for not following our rules.

At the Y, we pride ourselves on our ability to connect people. The cleverest introduction was by a ninety-two-year-old member who introduced himself as "honey" to an attractive female member. Every time she greeted him, she would say, "Hello, Honey."

Rule number one: if you are going to take a shower at the Y, then you should bring a towel to dry off. Standing at our paper-towel dispenser and unraveling twenty feet at a time to dry your body is unacceptable. It's a waste of paper, and it really beats up the handle mechanism. Also, the wall mounted hair dryers should be used only to dry the hair on your head.

All treadmills have cup holders. They are used for cups, water bottles, and drinks. In a pinch, you can roll up a magazine to keep it secure. The bottom of the cup holder is not designated to hold your gum, mints, or Life Savers.

Please don't shave all your body hair with an electric razor while standing naked in front of the mirror in the men's locker room having a conversation about yesterday's Yankees game. It just isn't right.

FaceTime technology is extraordinary. Using FaceTime in the locker room to speak to your mother while other women are changing into their workout gear is criminal.

Swim evaluations for your children are done in person, in our pool, with our trained swim instructor. Please don't send a video of your child swimming in your backyard pool and ask us to evaluate his or her swimming ability.

Please don't try to fake us out and alternate twin daughters in our swim lessons if you only paid for one child. It's obvious that their swimming abilities and names are different.

"Oh, I'm so sorry; I didn't recognize you in clothes." This is often said when members bump into one another out in the community. What they really mean to say is "I've only ever seen you sweaty, with no makeup, and in shorts and a T-shirt at the Y."

Sometimes I simply want a couple of minutes to use the urinal. Just because I am quietly staring at the wall uninterrupted does not give you permission to pepper me with questions. When you do, I will be as polite as I usually am—but I will not be able to make direct eye contact with you.

Walking from the wet area of the locker room to the dry area of the locker room without first drying yourself off after a shower is a big deal, especially when another member who's late for work steps in your puddle of water with a new pair of dry socks on. You haven't lived until a member comes charging down the hall in a wet pair of socks to complain.

Shooting baby powder from waist high onto your feet makes it appear like you're standing in your own private mini snowstorm. As if that's not bad enough, a three-foot wide circle of powder is now on the floor with your footprint squarely in the middle. I'm left with a complete mess on an otherwise clean floor, and the second you leave the locker room, two things inevitably happen: (1) it appears to others that the maintenance department hasn't cleaned the floor in a week, and (2) a member inadvertently steps in it with his or her bare feet and goes absolutely ballistic. You can only guess who that person is looking for when he or she gets dressed and exits.

My conflict resolution skills were seriously tested when a member was clipping his toenails on a bench and one shot three feet and hit another member in the eyelid. Livid wouldn't begin to describe the member who was assaulted by the flying toenail. Let's face it: clipping toenails should be done only in the privacy of your own home or at a doctor's office.

The Random Reality of Working at the YMCA

20
Reality

CORINNE, A THIRTY-FIVE-YEAR veteran YMCA professional once told me that if there is no chaos, then it's not a Y. She's right. Schedules, meetings, strategic planning, financial statements, reports, insurance, emergency first aid, building maintenance, people, interruptions, weather, children, families, adults, seniors, different languages, classes, programs, workshops, special events, personnel issues, permits, certifications, licenses, and more interruptions are part of the job every day.

In the course of any given chaotic day, among all that I do, making time to build sincere relationships with members is all-important. Every day becomes its own challenge and takes on a life of its own. Although every day begins with a plan, most of the time that plan changes, so the need to prioritize and balance hour by hour is essential. I organize each day and then reorganize each day. I balance each day and then rebalance each day. I realize that there's no substitute for patience and flexibility; otherwise, I will simply be ineffective.

My personal mantra each day is simple: organize it, embrace it, and kick its ass with a smile. It's probably a great rule for all workplaces, but especially at the Y. I thrive on making things happen. It keeps me energized, motivated, and passionate. Someone once told me that if you want something done, then connect with people who get things done, and I agree wholeheartedly. I do all I can to surround myself with Y people who get it done.

The reality is that helping others and working in a non-profit takes an enormous amount of time, sincere belief in your mission, and a personal belief that you are making a difference. Every day is not sunshine and butterflies. I am not building widgets; I am changing lives. I embrace my work. I embrace the fact that it's hard and that it's important and that I am blessed to have found this as my career. I embrace the fact that it can be mentally exhausting. It's where I learned the difference between physical exhaustion and mental exhaustion. When I was in high school, my dad used to say, "Use your brain until it hurts." I never really understood what it felt like for my brain to hurt because I never really studied in high school. I now understand what he meant.

My job is twenty-four/seven, 365 days a year. Whether I am in the Y building or out in the community, I am working. I am representing an organization that responds to community needs, reaches out to others, and makes a difference in people's lives. I organize it, I embrace it, and I kick its ass with a smile.

21
Slammed

KATHY UNLOCKED HER front door, entered her house, dropped her bags, tossed her keys on the table, and fell on the couch completely drained of energy. At some point, I'm sure that everyone who has ever worked hard has arrived home and said, "What a day." What they really meant was that they were so busy and mentally slammed by the demands of their jobs that they were emotionally and physically exhausted. Kathy had had one of those days.

In the morning, she consoled two women who had lost their husbands. Sue, a great friend of Kathy's, had enjoyed tremendous personal success over the past year by losing nearly seventy pounds, only to then be diagnosed with cancer. She beat the cancer only to find out that her husband of thirty-seven years also had cancer. She stopped by this day to tell Kathy that he had passed away. It was such a difficult conversation, but Kathy admired Sue's strength and appreciation for all the time she had spent with her loving husband. On the same day, Kathy learned that another dear friend, Geneva, was on her way into the procedure room for a minor surgical procedure only to find out that her husband had a massive stroke and died in the waiting room before her procedure even began. You really never know what a day will bring.

In the afternoon, Kathy decided to work out to relieve some mental stress and to get ready for the second half of her day. She stepped on the treadmill next to Clara, an eighty-three-year-old senior friend of hers. Clara told her a story of how her identity was stolen. She never owned a computer and never ordered anything online, and now her credit was put into collection for purchases she supposedly made from a variety of department stores. She also has a heart condition and severe arthritis. Kathy's heart broke for her misfortune. Clara thanked her for listening.

Late afternoon rolled around, and Kathy entered her office to a barrage of voicemails from members who were very upset with the new pool schedule that began that day. One by one, she returned each call but failed to appease anyone. The very people who pay her salary were verbally beating her up. She found it hard to keep their complaints in perspective given the day's earlier events.

After sitting in a classic New Jersey traffic jam, Kathy arrived home to find that her dog had gotten sick on the carpet and would need to see a veterinarian. Finally, she crawled into bed, and her last thought as she drifted off to sleep was that she's fortunate to have such a good life and that she really does enjoy her job.

22
Stilts

THE YMCA IS built to respond to certain community needs. A simple example is after-school childcare. There was a time not too long ago when there was always a parent home when the children arrived after school. Now that two-parent working families are the norm, school-age childcare became a common community issue. In local communities across the country, the YMCA stepped in to provide affordable, safe, and fun care for children, right at their local schools, until the parents came from work to pick them up. The positive impact is obvious—instead of children home alone, they are in a healthy, safe, and structured environment. Ys are sustained and thrive when they come together with the community to coordinate and show care for community needs.

A big part of my job is to be engaged in community activities while keeping my finger on the pulse of community needs. In other words, the community has to know us, and we have to know it.

One such annual activity that places the Y directly in front of the people we serve is our annual participation in the Fourth of July parade. It's a great way of showcasing the YMCA in a lighthearted and fun event. Seems simple, right? Get a few Y representatives, make a float, drive slowly, and wave to those men, women, and children lined along the street waving flags while wearing red, white, and blue. It's always simple until it's not. I've participated in dozens of parades representing the Y, but there is one particular Fourth of July parade where I found myself preventing a conflict between clowns and mermaids.

The YMCA parade float was behind an antique Good Humor ice-cream truck and in front of the local playhouse float, which featured *The Little Mermaid*. Following along to my right was the ever-entertaining and prominent man on stilts. There were about sixty different floats in the annual Fourth of July parade, and the YMCA had an excellent position at number twenty-three.

Halfway into the parade, I noticed the man on stilts spending a lot of time near the Good Humor man. In fact, he was sitting in the front seat of the Good Humor truck such that his long stilt legs were overhanging the front hood of the truck. From time to time, he would stand up and entertain the crowd, but then he would immediately sit back down with the Good Humor man.

We continued on, until suddenly my section of the parade stopped, and clowns started surrounding my YMCA float. A panicked lead clown, complete with the big, red, painted-on smile, the white face makeup, the red bushy hair, the red bubble nose, and the heavy wool clown outfit, approached my window to tell me that the man on stilts was suffering heatstroke. He went on to explain that the Good Humor man was going to race the man on stilts to the rescue squad stationed a quarter mile away. The small army of clowns would be taking the place of the Good Humor man in front of my truck, but I was instructed to give them plenty of space so that the children behind me, who were singing *The Little Mermaid* song, didn't interfere with the clowns singing in front of me.

To recap, I'm in a Fourth of July parade representing the YMCA, I'm watching the man on stilts go down from heatstroke and the Good Humor man come to the rescue, I'm negotiating with a panicked big-red-nose clown, and my job is to hold back the mermaids so that the army of clowns can dance and sing without being drowned out by *The Little Mermaid* song. Serious pressure. OK—got it.

I was literally caught in the middle, but I am happy to report that I did my job, and I kept the peace between the army of clowns and the mermaids.

23
Job Descriptions

CONSIDERING ALL THE random situations we find ourselves in daily that are absolutely unrelated to our existing job descriptions, Kathy and I have a running joke: "Hey, not doing it! That's not in my job description!"

After a particularly challenging day, via an e-mail, Kathy proposed a new job description for herself as aquatics director.

- Aquatics director general function: the aquatics director reports directly to the CEO and every member who pays a membership fee.
- Job specification: the incumbent must have appropriate academic preparation with major emphasis and experience in aquatics. If you don't take initiative and are reactive instead of proactive, then you won't have a long career.

- Job segments: responsible for the supervision of pool maintenance and meeting all safety and sanitation requirements as well as all local and state codes and regulations governing pools. If someone poops in the pool, clean it. If someone vomits in the pool, clean it. Band-Aids, clean it. Hair, clean it. If someone jumps in without a bathing suit on, tell them to get out.
- Assure safety, function, and cleanliness of the department, which includes the entirety of the YMCA facility, not just the pool. If someone blows off his or her toenail by dropping a dumbbell on it in the free weight area, which is as far away as you can get from the pool while still being in the same building, then expect to be the one cleaning the person up. After all, you are the highest trained emergency first-aid responder in the building.
- Develop a team of professionals to deliver high-quality aquatic programs on a tight budget. Hiring lifeguards is really hard because the job is really boring. Until it's not.
- Expect half of your staff to have a crying fit once per week. Expect the other half of your staff to be late for their shifts.
- Demonstrate maturity and good judgment. Have excellent human-relations skills, and don't flip out when some kid's mother is screaming at you so loudly that your eardrums are bleeding.

- Plan and develop the annual aquatics budget with the CFO, and pretend you understand what he or she is talking about because you have absolutely no financial background.
- Any and all other responsibilities that are deemed necessary to the full functionality of the Y.

• • •

It's actually a realistic description of her life as an aquatics director.

24
A Real Job Interview

YMCA JOB INTERVIEWS are always entertaining, and I am at the point where, as soon as the applicant walks into my office and starts incessantly talking, I feel like yelling, "Enough talking! Just show me how good you are."

It's time to rethink the traditional job interview. You always learn more by watching and listening than by talking.

Place your new youth sports applicant in a gymnasium with a red bouncy ball, fifteen children, and no directions as soon as he or she arrives for the interview. A qualified youth sports instructor should be able to keep them moving and entertained while teaching them something new for forty-five minutes.

As soon as your new preschool child care applicant walks through the front door, sit the candidate in a small chair at a small table with three-year-olds who are eating Cheez-Its and drinking grape juice. A qualified preschool child-care worker will have a great time with the children and learn everyone's names within fifteen minutes.

As soon as you meet, ask your potential new school-age child-care worker to sit cross-legged on the floor in a circle with third graders to guide them in a game of Duck Duck Goose. He or she should have the kids laughing and all participating for fifteen minutes.

Meet your potential new aquatics director candidate at a busy town pool. Make sure that he or she is facing the pool and that you are facing away from the pool. Talk about everything except aquatics. If you have a delightful conversation and he or she makes excellent eye contact, then the candidate probably is not qualified. A really good aquatics director should be uncomfortable and fidgety while looking over your shoulder at the pool, scanning for unsafe situations.

Ask your potential new facilities manager if he or she is available for an interview at 3:00a.m. on a Sunday morning. If the person doesn't hesitate and replies, "Sure, no problem," then he or she is most likely a great candidate.

Meet your potential new frontline customer service agent behind the front desk at the busiest time of the day. Make an excuse and leave him or her behind the desk for fifteen minutes. If the candidate is smiling and engaging customers on his or her own, then the person will probably be a good employee. If the candidate is standing in the same exact spot where you left him or her, then you should make it a short interview.

25
I Made a Mistake

I CAN TEACH twenty-five fourth graders in a basketball clinic, and each and every one of them will listen, learn, and have a great time. The same goes for T-ball, soccer, and every youth fitness program imaginable. I was "that guy" at the Y whom mothers and fathers wanted as a coach for their school-age children. If I had a penny for every time a parent complimented me after a clinic or a class, then I would have retired when I was thirty. And then it happened. It was the first day of a new basketball clinic, and I was teaching twenty-five third-grade girls and boys how to pass, dribble, and shoot. After about twenty minutes of a forty-five minute class, little Johnny decided he would rather throw basketballs, tease his friends, and goof off than participate in the basketball clinic. Been there, done that. I gave little Johnny a five-minute time-out and sat him in the far corner of the gymnasium. A little time to cool off usually works well. When the clinic ended, I began the process of returning children safely to their parents. I was making small talk with a parent when I noticed little Johnny's mother looking for her son. It was then that it dawned on me: I had forgotten Johnny was in timeout. I glanced over to the corner of the gym, and little third-grade Johnny was crying hysterically. I had left him sitting in timeout for twenty-five minutes. I was mortified, and little Johnny's mom was very upset. She tore me up and down for three straight minutes without me saying a single word. During those three minutes, I remember thinking about all kinds of excuses with which I was going to defend myself. Finally, when it was my turn to speak, I said only one sentence: "It was my fault; I made a bad mistake, and I'm really sorry." We stared at each other for what seemed like five minutes but was probably only five seconds, and that was it: the conversation was over, and Mom took little Johnny home.

I felt horrible, especially since I was so new at the Y and wanted to make a good impression. I was certain that I would be suspended or fired. I arrived at work the next morning with the situation weighing heavily on my mind, and sure enough, there was a note on my desk from my boss wanting to talk to me. To say that my heart sank would be an understatement. I figured I'd be fired that day. I entered my boss's office, and he had a big smile on his face. He said, "I just talked to little Johnny's mom, and you made quite an impression on her." I forgot exactly what I said, but I'm sure I sounded like a bumbling idiot. "Johnny's mom was really upset about the situation in the basketball clinic but really appreciated your honesty in responding to her. She respected that you made no excuses, you admitted your mistake, and you owned it. She also wants you to know that little Johnny will be at the clinic next week."

Life lesson learned.

26
The Journey

CHILDREN NEED TO fail, and children need to succeed, and I'd like to think that, at its very best, the Y allows that to happen.

Every parent wants a child who becomes a responsible, productive part of society and has healthy self-esteem. From my experience at the Y, the more capable a child is at a young age, the greater the chance that the child becomes a self-confident, independent, and productive member of society as he or she gets older. Children feel capable and build confidence when they accomplish a goal or complete a task. Heck, I feel capable and confident when I accomplish a goal or complete a task. We all do. A five-year-old does not need help answering a simple question from an adult. A nineteen-year-old's mother should not be calling me to arrange community service for her son. A nine-year-old does not need help zipping up her jacket and putting on her hat. An eleven-year-old does not need help putting a dollar in the vending machine.

One of the reasons swimming lessons are so good for children at a young age is because they learn a new skill, and they do it themselves. A good YMCA swim instructor simply gives gentle guidance while the young children master the skill and figure it out for themselves. Learning to swim is secondary; the confidence that they build in themselves because they learned something new is primary. Have you ever watched a five-year-old try to shoot a basketball through the hoop on a ten-foot basket? I've watched children shoot for a half hour straight and never hit the rim, but they keep trying.

I maintain that every single shot they take and miss is every bit as important as the one that goes in. The journey can be long and grueling, but it's where they learn. The journey is where confidence is built. Allow the journey to happen, and allow them to embrace it.

Once the goal is reached, it lasts only for a fleeting moment. The journey will begin again.

It's never about the goal; it's always about the journey.

27
It's Not Rocket Science

PACK A GYM bag in the morning, drive to your exercise location, change into your workout clothes, figure out how to operate the equipment, and get sweaty. It's uncomfortable, it's intimidating, it's inconvenient, and you're really sore the next day. Then you are supposed to do it again tomorrow. Why would anyone in his or her right mind pay for that?

Most people simply aren't motivated to exercise. I can spot a new member in seconds simply by the way he or she wanders aimlessly through our maze of exercise equipment.

Conservatively, over the last thirty years, I've talked to five hundred people who join the Y and want to start an exercise program. Inevitably, they tell me one of two things: (1) my goal is to lose weight, or (2) my goal is to get in shape. To that I always respond, "No, that's not your goal. Your goal is to drive into our parking lot and walk through the front door."

For those who do exercise, you understand how it improves your attitude, how it improves your overall energy, and how it's a great environment in which to network and meet new friends. In my case, I now realize that I exercise more for what's above my neck than below it. If I miss a workout, then I just don't feel right. All people who exercise regularly would agree with that.

You really don't have to join anywhere to exercise and feel great. Put on your sneakers and take a walk. When those walks get too easy, take a longer walk, and add a hill. And when that gets too easy, add an abdominal routine, and do some push-ups. You'll get in shape, and you'll feel great. And finally, you have to eat right. Everyone knows what that means. Trust me; it's not rocket science.

I'm the CEO of a YMCA, and I just told you that you don't have to join to exercise. Why should you join the YMCA? The social aspect of being part of a YMCA is why people join and the main reason people keep coming back. A dear friend and senior member, Tom, once told me that our $435 membership rate is a great deal: "The way I look at it is that I pay two hundred dollars a year to exercise and two hundred thirty-five dollars a year to bullshit with my friends." He's been a member more than fifteen years.

28
Don't Stop

SALLY, A MARRIED thirty-seven-year-old mother of two and cancer survivor, gave me a lot to think about one day. She said, "Ever notice how many people stop taking care of themselves when they need it most? My husband and I worked out regularly five days a week, my blood tests were perfect, my career was going great, my children were doing well in school, and it was a seventy-and-sunny day when I found out I had cancer. It's just so easy to feel great when important things in your life are aligned and well. Then life happened."

I know a lot of people from all walks of life. In fact, I know so many people so well that I've memorized their routines and their exercise schedules. Not because I purposely try to but because I've been working at the Y so long. Quite often, I notice when someone stops arriving at his or her typical time, and I reach out to that person.

Inevitably, I get the same basic response: "I'd love to be there, but I'm just too busy and have no time" or "I'm just not feeling well these days."

I've noticed that when stressful periods start, many people begin to ignore basic needs. Ironically, it's during the crisis when you most need to take care of yourself and be at your best; however, many people do the complete opposite. Once the decision is made that your needs are unimportant, the bad habits creep in. This is the exact point in time that the vicious unhealthy cycle begins. Unfortunately, I've seen it a hundred times. The original YMCA idea is that health is a very personal balance between your mind, your body, and your spirit. It's easy to attain balance when all is well, yet it is easily forgotten when life becomes messy.

I've had a lot of teachers, but what Sally said to me that day changed me. I remember clearly that during her battle with cancer, and especially for the duration of her chemotherapy, she made every effort to come to the Y. When she was too weak to exercise, she simply socialized with her Y friends. Either way, even at her lowest moment, she always made it a point to somehow strengthen herself physically and emotionally each day. She ultimately beat cancer, and I believe her attitude had everything to do with it.

I know many others with the same type of story as Sally's. I've noticed they all have the same dynamic aura about them. They could easily use the "too busy" or "not feeling well" excuse, but they choose not to. Without even knowing it, these people are inspirational simply by the way they live and the choices they make.

29
Flowered Bathing Caps

I SAY AQUATIC fitness, and you think of elderly women in flowered bathing caps dancing around in a pool to big-band music from the 1940s. Getting people to understand the benefits of aquatic fitness is like trying to explain to someone how to solve the Rubik's Cube—it just can't be done. You simply must pick up the Rubik's Cube and start twisting. It's the same with aquatic fitness—you simply must get in the pool and try it. I've seen miracles occur in our pools. I've watched people enter the Y in a wheelchair and *run* on our treadmill in the water. I've watched people enter the Y holding on dearly to a metal walker for support and participate in aquatic volleyball. I've watched tense special needs children become calm and relaxed in the water. I see miracles every day, and it never gets old.

If you've ever had the luxury of rehabbing an injury in the pool, then you'll never understand why anyone rehabs on land. It's that good. It's that remarkable. Without getting into too much science, I'll break it down to its simplest form. With water about chest high, you are approximately 70 percent lighter than you are on land. You also become much more flexible. Simply by standing in the water, the pressure of the water around you benefits your muscles. Sounds too good to be true, right? Admittedly, aquatic people are different from everyone else. They are a quirky bunch. A bathing suit in public? Not a problem. Chlorine-bleached hair? Who cares? The extra time it takes to dry off and get ready for the workday? Big deal. I'm convinced there are two types of people: water people and land people. Kathy, of course, is in the water people category, and I am in the land people category. I thought of water like most land people probably do: lap swimming or goofing around with my children at a backyard pool or the beach. I became a water believer when I rehabbed an old ankle injury to 100 percent using some vertical water exercises that Kathy gave me.

Kathy taught me and many others that if you want to feel better on land, then train in the water. Land people probably won't believe me. But if by some chance you are out of options and you really want to heal, then come see me, and I'll connect you with Kathy.

30
Following the Crowd

SOMETIMES I DO stupid things, and it's probably because I'm human. It took me a while to accept that. Each day at the Y, the walking/running direction changes on our indoor track. Every other day, you either walk clockwise or counterclockwise. Simple.

One day, I entered the track, and I saw eight people walking clockwise, and one middle-aged woman walking counterclockwise. In my typical kind and gentle fashion, I approached the one woman walking counterclockwise to explain the track directional rules. As I walked around the track talking to her, the conversation went like this:

"Hi. I'm Bill, and I work here. I just want to let you know that the direction of the track is clockwise today," I said with a big smile and in a friendly tone.

Without breaking stride she said, "Are you sure?"

"Yes, I'm sure. Would you mind reversing direction and walking in the same direction as the rest?"

"Yes, I would mind."

"Why?"

"Because you're wrong."

"How am I wrong? Look at the rest of the members."

"I'm the only one who read the proper direction to walk on the track today." She was right, and the eight other people on the track and I were wrong.

I've always prided myself on not following the crowd, and that day I did. She taught me that situations are not always as they seem. She taught me that, before I attempt conflict resolution, I need to know all the facts.

.

31
Valentine's Day

BOOM. WHILE THE pool was packed with swimmers, it sounded like someone had pulled the trigger on a twelve-gauge shotgun. Thankfully, it wasn't a shotgun, but it had the potential to be worse. One of the ten main beams that hold up the pool roof had suddenly cracked. Fortunately, the beam remained in place, but my fear was that it would let go, and the roof would collapse into the pool. We stayed calm, cleared the pool, and evacuated the Y before anyone was hurt. Staff did a marvelous job. Within twenty minutes, everyone was out, and the Y was closed. It was 4:00 p.m. on a freezing cold Friday after two days of heavy snow—and it happened to be Valentine's Day. After the beam broke and the Y was evacuated, I knew I was in for a long haul. The most amazing sequence of events would follow. Rich, the aquatics supervisor on duty who witnessed the event, Kathy, and the other leadership staff met, and we put our plan in motion. Our biggest concern was to prevent the roof from collapsing. Rich and I would stay, while everyone else would go home. It certainly wasn't the Valentine's Day either of us had planned.

In the meantime, the beam continued to crack, sounding a lot like a tree slowly cracking as it is about to fall. It was an eerie sound, and we were facing an ominous situation.

The first call was to a board member who was also the town engineer. He placed a call to a friend of his who is a structural engineer. The structural engineer happened to be a half hour away, heading toward another client, when he received our call. He turned his car around to come evaluate our situation. Arriving by 5:00p.m., the structural engineer had a plan in place by 6:00p.m. for temporary support of the beam by using special scaffolding and columns. Incredibly, we located the proper scaffolding and the people to install it that night. As luck would have it, their main headquarters was only one town over. They were on site by 10:00p.m., changed into a pair of shorts or stripped down to their underwear, and entered the pool to begin installation of the massive scaffolding and columns while the pool was slowly being drained. By 4:00 a.m., twelve hours after our Valentine's Day plans had taken a turn for the worse, a heavy metal frame secured the pool beam, and the danger of imminent collapse was minimized. Research now began for the long-term solution to our beam problem. There are only a few companies in the country that make repairs to these specific types of laminated beams. Lucky yet again, one of the repair companies that services the entire United States is located about forty miles away in Hackensack, New Jersey, and they just happened to be on a job site only a few miles from us. Somehow, I convinced them to meet us the next day. A few days later, we obtained permission from the town to open the Y for business, while the pool remained closed for repairs. Six weeks later, the pool reopened, and we were 100 percent back in business. One week after the roof repair was completed, we were evaluating the significant loss of program income because of the beam break when we received a surprise donation for $330,000 from a dear friend who had passed away months before and left us in his will. A repair like this could've easily taken six months, but instead it took six weeks. This could've been a devastating loss for the Y, but instead it became a story about teamwork, dedication, perseverance, and luck. For me, it validated what I already knew to be true. Life happens fast whether you're ready or not. My Valentine's Day plans did not include a broken beam, nor could I have thought in my wildest imagination that I'd be spending it with Rich. I should remember to send him a card next Valentine's Day.

32
Bartending and the YMCA

ALTHOUGH I HAD many part-time jobs in college, bartending is what paid the bills, and little did I know back then that it would be a great training ground for my long career at the Y. I tended bar from 3:00 p.m. until I closed after midnight. It was a great shift because it was busy, and I was the bartender people came to see right after work and before going home. I knew everyone by name; I knew what drink to serve them as well as an awful lot about their personal lives. Honestly, my motivation for getting to know my customers well was purely to maximize my tips.

As a young college kid, I learned a lot from listening to my customers about the stresses of work, relationships, and raising a family because, inevitably, as I was serving drinks, that's all they would ever talk about. I remember one middle-aged man named Ray. He worked ten hours a day in the local lumberyard and would arrive at 4:15 p.m. Monday through Friday. He walked slowly, shoulders slumped, and never had a smile; he would simply sit down and mumble an order for a Rolling Rock. It got to the point that the minute he opened the door, I would crack open a Rolling Rock and put it near an empty bar stool. He wouldn't say a word to me until after his second beer, and then the conversation flowed. Ray came to the bar and used alcohol and conversation with me to take the edge off from a hard day at work before he went to see his family. He always left happier and more relaxed than when he arrived.

Fast-forward fifteen years, and I realized that regular Y members are not much different from Ray. They simply make a different choice, a healthy choice. Likewise, working at the front desk of the YMCA is not much different from tending bar. At prime time after work, hundreds of people enter the Y. Many have already had a long, hard day at work, sat in rugged New Jersey traffic, and are simply coming to the Y to take the edge off by exercising or participating in a program before they go home to see their families or take their children to little-league practice.

One of the hardest things to teach people who work at the Y is to not "own" someone else's feelings. Happy, sad, mean, or angry, I think it's human nature to mirror another person's attitude. It's all too easy to be friendly to someone who's nice and defensive to someone who's angry. In staff trainings, I always emphasize the point that you just don't know. We simply never know what may be going on in a person's life that causes him or her to be sad, grumpy, or mean when he or she enters the Y. I like to think that our job at the Y is to provide a peaceful, positive oasis from the rough outside world, and it always starts with a friendly staff. Life is tough, and many members enter the Y just as Ray used to enter the bar after work, stressed and out of sorts. It's astonishing, though, that one hour later that same grumpy, out-of-sorts Y member will often leave content and ready to take on the rest of his or her day. I give that member a lot of credit for choosing exercise over alcohol.

33
The Suggestion Box

I HAVE A suggestion box. Members can call, text, or e-mail me anytime, but many people still like to leave hand-written messages on scrap paper in my little suggestion box at the front desk. All are encouraged to leave their names, phone numbers, and e-mail addresses so that I can contact them to discuss their suggestions. It seems prehistoric, but it's a great communication tool.

Suggestions are sometimes made without any way of responding back because the member fails to leave his or her contact information. Here are some of my all-time favorite suggestions, along with how I may have responded had they left their contact information.

More options for the vending machine: soup, chicken.

I'm looking into that. I'm also looking into pasta fagioli, split-pea soup, and prime rib.

Dear Barbell Blast instructor—you killed me on Monday, and I love it! Thanks.

I'm so sorry to hear that. We'll meet on the other side.

Vending machines. You have fiber bars for the old-timers, how about protein bars for the weightlifters? Makes sense, right?

It does make sense. Just so you know, a diet high in fiber is beneficial to all ages.

Hi, my name is idk.

Hi, idk. I'm Bill. Nice to meet you.

Give us a diving board now!

Sorry, I can't do that because I wouldn't be able to afford the insurance premium unless I triple your membership fees.

Please add Skittles to the vending machine so I can taste the rainbow.

Will do. I'm also adding a Coke and a smile.

Valet parking and laundry service.

Would be nice, but your membership rate will double.

The window in babysitting is broken and not opening properly and I didn't do it.

Oh, yes, you did!

We would like a carport in the back of the building for my Charger and my girlfriend's Accord. We think this will help keep the cars looking good. Thanks.

I'm on it. I'll let you know when it's built.

The pool is currently 82°. Please make it 83°.

I'm on it. You are exactly right.

I think the scale in the men's locker room is 2 pounds off. Last Wednesday I weighed 170, and a week later I weighed 172.

I tested it, and it is calibrated perfectly. It must mean that you ate more calories than you burned last week.

Color-coordinate the treadmills.

What does that even mean?

Put a "do not spit in the water fountain" sign to stop people from spitting in the water fountain.

Only people who are already following the rules read what's written on the signs.

The new jump ropes are sublime! They are so nice that I stole two of them today.

Thanks for letting me know. Your fingerprints were all over the suggestion note that you left me, and the local police will be contacting you soon.

I enjoyed my class in the pool but ran out of water.

How is that possible?

Circus-style tent for sale, $2,000.

I may be interested. Can I come see it?

I just worked my way up to the number four rubber band, but there are none left on the floor. I can't go back to those sissy bands.

Signed the rubber band man.

Thanks for letting me know, and nice to meet you, rubber band man.

The music downstairs is not appropriate music to work out to. Captain and Tennille and Air Supply are more acceptable at a dentist's office than at a YMCA.

Can't argue with that; I'll change the station immediately.

Thanks for the wife.

I think you meant Wi-Fi.

It's cold in the parking lot in the mornings. Afternoons are OK. Please handle.

OK. Wait, what do you want me to handle?

I just want to let you know that Donna did an excellent job assisting my sister while she almost fainted. Her expertise, ability to communicate, and composure were very impressive; she deserves a huge pat on the back. Thank you.

Glad everything is OK!

Please consider publicizing that the YMCA should be fragrance free. Some people arrive who are heavily perfumed.

I've never heard of that. Is that even a thing?

Can you please have the spinning instructor STOP singing during class? We can't sing to ourselves or think straight due to her singing.

I think it's great.

I'm upset because a woman was giving herself an oatmeal mask at the sink, and another one was washing her armpits. Please put a sign to keep people from doing private things in the locker room.

I will, as soon as I stop laughing. The visual is just too funny.

I saw a honeybee in the men's locker room.

That's nothing. One time, I saw a praying mantis.

Peel me a grape.

Reading your suggestion was how I imagined stepping into the twilight zone would be.

How can we develop a policy where men should cover their armpits? I'm seriously grossed out.

That would probably be a tough one to enforce, especially in the pool.

I snuck two people into the Y today.

Thanks for telling me. I probably have it on camera, but either way, I hope they join.

I am very concerned that we no longer have Life Savers at the front desk. Please solve this issue, or I will be forced to relocate.

The Y is here to serve, and by serve, we don't necessarily mean Life Savers. But they are certainly cheap enough, so I will reinstate the bag of Life Savers at the front desk.

34
Alaska

COMING OUT OF high school and dreading the idea of going to college, I tried to convince my parents that I either wanted to be a cross-country truck driver or work on a commercial fishing boat in Alaska. After all, I always got the same advice from high school guidance counselors, which was a combination of make sure you find a career you love and think of things you like to do and translate those into a career. I liked to drive, and I liked to fish, so logically, being a truck driver or a commercial fisherman sounded like a good idea—until, of course, I presented my future plans to my parents. Their suggestion was to go to college and decide after graduation. Of course I knew better, but I took their advice. I enrolled in three different colleges before I locked in and finished my bachelor's degree in physical education. Since I was a sports and fitness guy, a physical education degree seemed like a logical choice. I followed the traditional college route of fifteen to eighteen credits per semester, all aligned to receive my physical education degree in four years. Because I was responsible for paying my college tuition, I worked a combination of part-time jobs that translated into full-time hours all four years while attending school. I can make the case that I learned as much from my part-time jobs as I did in the college classroom. Bartending, lumberyard, gas station, cook, dishwasher—you name it, and I probably did it.

My college internship at a youth correctional facility and a youth shelter had the greatest impact on me. At this point, you're probably thinking, *how, exactly, did you end up in a correctional facility and a youth shelter with a physical education degree?* Simple. They were located near each other, and they both needed a sports guy to supervise and coach the kids, develop programs, and keep them busy and out of trouble. I can't pinpoint a moment in time when I realized I had a talent for working with kids, but I do know it was during this internship that I realized I was making a difference in these young people's lives. It motivated me. Every day, I was either working with kids who were locked up or literally homeless if not for the shelter. Through the programs, exercise, and made-up competitive games, I provided a positive physical outlet for them, and they enjoyed it. After completing my college internship and graduating college, I stayed on as an employee at the youth correctional facility. I really wanted to make it a career...until the day I realized it would never amount to one that would pay the bills.

Then my "real" job search began.

Looking for a solid career after college was much more difficult than I had anticipated. I focused my job search toward sports management—after all, I had a physical education degree and had taken some courses in management, and it seemed like a solid plan. Working with youth seemed like a dead-end type of career, and I felt management had a significant upside. I was offered career opportunities in "sports management," but there was no way I was making a livelihood out of a Foot Locker athletic shoe store or Rock and Bowl, so as hope dwindled, I seriously reconsidered my original plan of becoming a cross-country truck driver or commercial fisherman in Alaska. At one point, I was so distraught with my job search that I literally mailed a résumé with a coffee stain and no cover letter for a position I'd read about in a local newspaper for a nautilus director at a nearby YMCA. At the time, nautilus exercise equipment was innovative strength-training machines for every major muscle group and, for the first time, made resistance training appealing to the general public. This particular YMCA had a room dedicated to the nautilus equipment and needed a person to oversee it. I was familiar with the exercise machines, had a college degree, and was confident that I was qualified for the job.

I had absolutely no knowledge of what the YMCA was about when I applied; however, I was encouraged by the brief research I did before my interview. To my surprise, the Y combined much of what I was looking for: fitness, youth programs, management opportunities, and a career path. I did feel at a slight disadvantage going in because I had never been a YMCA kid: I had never gone to YMCA camp, and I hadn't learned to swim at the YMCA. In fact, I had never stepped foot in a YMCA until my job interview.

I'll never know if my interview was luck or destiny, but I was hired on the spot. It wasn't long before my role as nautilus director expanded into teaching all the youth programs. I was also encouraged and took advantage of all the opportunities to network, train, and develop my career as a YMCA professional. After only a couple of years, I knew I wanted to be "that guy" in charge of the Y.

Today, I dedicate an enormous amount of time to the YMCA—in fact, my whole family does. But to this day, the YMCA continues to teach me more than I ever imagined. I learned not to underestimate my potential to make a difference by helping others and at the same time live the life I want. I learned to listen, and I learned that giving to those less fortunate is all-important. I recognize that no one has an easy journey and that it's important to embrace your own personal journey. I'm not afraid to be successful, but I'm also aware that success is very personal, and all that matters is how I define it. I learned how to roll with the punches, and I understand that plans change—plans always change.

But most of all, I realize that every day I have a choice.

About the Author

Bill Lamia began working at the YMCA in 1988 and worked his way up. He is now CEO of the YMCA in Randolph, New Jersey, and he is enthusiastic about the many ways the Y strengthens and supports both communities and individuals.

Lamia graduated from East Stroudsburg University in 1986. He lives in New Jersey with his wife and two daughters.

Made in the USA
Columbia, SC
23 January 2019